Smarter *than the* SCOOPERS

Keeping your child safe from predators!

published by

National Center for Youth Issues

Practical Guidance Resources
Educators Can Trust

ncyi.org

www.ncyi.org

This book is dedicated to Spencer, a true hero who NEVER gives up!
–Julia

Duplication and Copyright

National Center for Youth Issues
Practical Guidance Resources
Educators Can Trust

P.O. Box 22185
Chattanooga, TN 37422-2185
423.899.5714 • 866.318.6294
fax: 423.899.4547
www.ncyi.org

ISBN: 978-1-937870-07-2
© 2012 National Center for Youth Issues, Chattanooga, TN
All rights reserved.

Written by: Julia Cook
Illustrations by: Allison Valentine
Design by: Phillip W. Rodgers
Published by National Center for Youth Issues
Softcover

Printed at RR Donnelley • Reynosa, Tamaulipas, Mexico • July 2016

I was outside playing with Zippy, my new baby rabbit, when I heard my mama calling me.

3

I carefully set Zippy down into a cardboard box and ran inside the house to see what she wanted.

Mama made me sit down in the "Talk To" chair. Mama always has a lot to say, but when you have to sit down in the "Talk To" chair, you know what she's about to say is *very* important.

Mama said it was time for me to learn the "**Scooper Safety Rules**".

"People come in all shapes and sizes," said Mama.

"Some people are **large**; others are **scrawny**; some are tall; some are **short**."

"Some people have **BIG** hair; others have **NO** hair.

Some people look kinda strange , and others look just fine."

"Our world is full of SAFE PEOPLE that you can go to if you ever need help," said Mama.

"What does a safe person look like?" I asked.

"A SAFE PERSON can be a mama with children, a police officer, a fire fighter, a teacher, or a clerk working at a store...

Most people are nice and kind. But there are some people out there who are SCOOPERS. A SCOOPER is a person who scoops you up, takes you away from your family, and tries to hurt you. **A SCOOPER can be a person that you know or a person that you have never met before."**

"How can I tell?" I asked my mama. "How do I know if a person is a SCOOPER?"

"Well, you can't tell by looking at their outside," Mama said. "So you have to be SMART and trust your instincts."

"My what?"

"Your instincts, you know the 'UH OH' voices in your head that tell you when things aren't right."

Yesterday, my neighbor, Mrs. Bridgman, came to school to pick me up. My mama didn't tell me that was going to happen, so I would not leave with Mrs. Bridgman. I went back inside the school and used my "CALL LIST".

"You should never go with anybody unless you check them out with someone on your CALL LIST," said Mama.

A CALL LIST is a list of people that I can call to make sure that I am making the right choice. My CALL LIST has 3 people and their phone numbers on it: Mamma, Grandma, and Aunt Suzie. If a person ever says, "Hey, you need to go with me," and I'm not sure, I go to the nearest phone and use my CALL LIST. I'm always supposed to stay by the phone until I can get someone on my CALL LIST to answer.

First, I called my mama...no answer.

Then, I called my grandma...She answered and said it was just fine to ride home with Mrs. Bridgman, so I did.

That night, I told my mama what happened after school.

"I'm so proud of you for using your CALL LIST," she said. "Checking first is always the right thing to do."

"Well, I think you're just a big Fraidy Cat," said my big brother, Myron. "Besides, you're too much of a brat to get scooped up by a SCOOPER!"

"Oh no," said Mama. "You can never be too careful. Even brats can get scooped!"

"If a grown-up that you don't know tries to talk to you, and you are alone, you shouldn't talk back to him. You should ignore what he says and walk away. Grown-ups that you don't know very well shouldn't come up to you when you are by yourself and start talking to you. You never can tell," said Mama. "That grown-up just might be a SCOOPER!"

13

"How can I tell if I know a grown-up well enough to talk to him?" I asked.

"You can always talk to SAFE PEOPLE," said Mama. "But if you're not sure, use the *Dinner Guide.* Would I invite the person who is talking to you over for dinner? If not, ignore what he is saying and walk away."

"You need to be really careful when you are using the computer. Never get on the Internet without asking for permission. SCOOPERS use the Internet to trick kids into talking to them by pretending to be somebody else. Since you can't see the person you are talking to, it could be a trap! And you're too smart to get trapped!"

15

"A SCOOPER might pretend to need your help. He might knock on our front door and say something like, 'Hi, I'm looking for the Cook residence and my cell phone battery is dead. Can I come into your house for just a minute and use the phone?'"

"I would NEVER let anyone into our house unless you were there to say it's O.K.," I said. "I would ignore his knock and not talk to him at all."

"That's right," said Mama. "If that person really does need help, he can try another house where there's a grown-up at home."

" A SCOOPER needs your attention and might try to trick you into getting too close to her," said Mama. "She might say something like, 'Hey, see my new puppy, isn't he cute?' Then when you kneel down to pet the puppy, she might try to scoop you up and take you away from our family."

"No one can scoop you if they can't reach you," said Mama. "You have to keep people OUT of your personal space. The cute puppy could be a trap, and you're too smart for traps! You need to ignore what the person says to you and keep a safe distance."

"Personal Space is SO important! Always keep a safe distance!
And remember: No one can scoop you if they can't reach you!"

My mama never lets me play in the park by myself. I always have to pair up with someone. Usually, I go with my big brother, Myron. He's as strong as an ox!

A SCOOPER would have a tough time scooping up Myron. When Mama tries to pick him up, she says he's nailed to the floor. Besides, Myron's really smart. He has a great "Uh Oh" voice, and he knows the

SCOOPER SAFETY RULES!

"I wish all the SCOOPERS out there would wear name tags so I could tell who they were," I said.

"That would only happen in a perfect world," said Mama. "But if you use my five important **SCOOPER SAFETY RULES**, you'll be safe from scooping,"

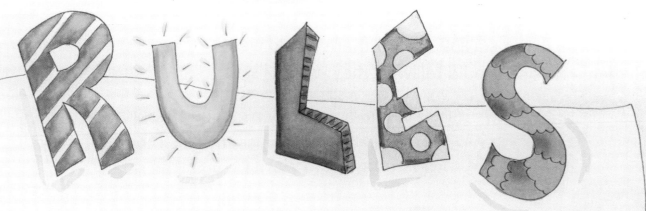

RULES

They are:

RULE #1 Be **SMART** and confident and trust your instincts. Always listen to your "Uh Oh" voice.

RULE #2 Never go with anyone without checking it out on your **CALL LIST.**

RULE #3 **ZerO Talking** to people that you don't know very well, especially when you are alone.

RULE #4 Keep people **OUT** of your personal space.

RULE #5 **Pair Up** when you go places so you are not alone.

"That's way too much for me to remember," I said.

"Oh, I can help you with that," said Mama.

She took a hold of my hand and with a marker, she wrote the word **SCOOP** on my finger tips.

"What's this for?" I asked.

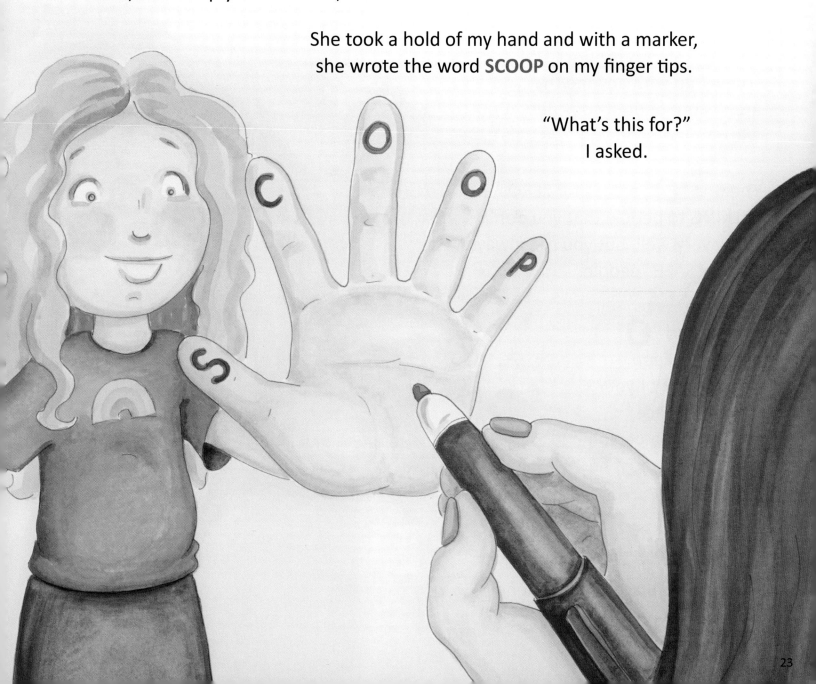

"Well, the "**S**" stands for BE SMART and listen to your "Uh Oh" voice.

The "**C**" stands for CALL LIST – never go with anyone that you aren't sure of until you check it out with someone on your CALL LIST.

The first "**O**" stands for ZERO TALKING to people that you don't know very well, but you can always talk to "SAFE" people.

The second "**O**" stands for Keep people OUT of your personal space. Remember, a person can't scoop you if he can't reach you!

And the "**P**" stands for PAIR UP – Always go places with a friend.

Mama smiled at me and gave me a great big hug.

"I love you so much," she said.

Then I went back outside and looked at the **SCOOP** on my finger tips, and I thought about everything my mama had said.

I looked inside the cardboard box. There he
was, my baby rabbit, my ZIPPY. He was perfect!
I'd planned on keeping him as a pet. I'd tricked him by
putting carrots in my backyard, and when he was busy eating,
I'd scooped him up and taken him away from his family. My tummy
started to get knots in it. To him,

I'd become a **SCOOPER!**

I carried the box to my backyard and set it down softly in the grass. I lifted my baby rabbit out of the box and held him up to my face. "I'm really sorry," I said, "for scooping you up and taking you away from your family."

I carefully set Zippy
down on the grass
and watched...

As he hopped back into the
bushes, right back to his
family, where he belongs.

A Note to Parents and Educators

There are some topics that we wish we never had to discuss with our children, abduction being one of them. Of course, we can choose to ignore the issue and simply hope it never happens. Another approach is to never let our children out of our sight. No one can advocate either of these strategies.

Most parents are eager to learn a simple and effective way to help protect their children from "Scoopers." When I was a child my parents told me not to take candy from strangers or get in a car with someone I didn't know. They had limited knowledge of this issue as did many other people. I can't ever remember hearing about a missing child as I was growing up. Today, the media have brought the issue to the public, for better, and for worse.

Parents constantly ask me, what do I need to do? Today, we need to empower our children with skills that will build their self-confidence in dealing with dangerous situations. We have to be careful not to tell our children that the world is full of scary people. Unfortunately, the news media do that for us. Rather, children need to know that most adults they encounter in their lives are basically good people. Parents and educators need to make child safety part of their everyday life by practicing and reviewing basic safety skills.

This book is an excellent way to start the dialogue and to open up our children's minds to the issue of luring prevention. Author Julia Cook has presented this subject in a manner that children will relate to. This book should be used as a tool to teach, renew, and practice the skills children need to know to keep them safe.

The child is usually the last line of defense against the "Scooper"!

Thanks, Julia for working with us to help keep our children safe!

Don Wood
Founder, Child Watch of North America

Safety Rules for Children

- Know your name, address, and phone number.

- Learn *how* and *when* to call 911.

- If you are scared of someone, RUN to safety.

- It's OK to be RUDE to a grown-up if you feel you are unsafe.

- Have a "Call List" and know how to use it.

- Don't let anyone on the phone or at the door know that you are home alone.

- If you ever get lost in a mall, stay where you are until you are found.

- Beware of an adult that asks you to keep a secret from your parents.

- Avoid shortcuts when you are walking from one place to another.

- If you are ever "scooped," scream, kick, bite, and fight as hard as you can to get away! Never ever trust what the "scooper" tells you.

- Tell your parents or a trusted adult if someone is asking you to do something that makes you feel uncomfortable. Listen to your "Uh Oh" voice.

- Always ask your parents for permission before getting on the Internet.

- Never talk to people online without your parent's permission.

- Review and practice these rules often.

Safety Rules for Parents

- Work hard to establish trust and communication with your children from day one!
- Don't ever leave children unattended in a vehicle, whether it is running or not.
- Make sure you know how to find or contact your children at all times.
- Take an active role in your children's activities.
- As tired as you may be, take the time to listen intently to your children when they tell you they had a bad dream. There could be a reason. Trust your instincts.
- Talk to your children about inappropriate incidences you hear on the news and get their perspective.
- Question and monitor anyone who takes an unusual interest in your children.
- Teach your children that they can be rude to an adult if they feel threatened in any way. They need to hear it from you directly because this message often contradicts everything they have heard before.
- Teach your children the difference between an "OK" secret and a "NOT OK" secret. Assure your children that you would never want him/her to feel like they had to keep a "NOT OK" secret from you.
- Have your children practice their most annoying scream. They may need to use it someday.
- Check websites for registered offenders in your neighborhood. Talk to your children about why these people should be avoided.
- Keep your family computer in a central location that is easily monitored.
- Avoid letting your children have Internet access in unsupervised areas. (i.e. computers in their bedrooms, etc.)
- Practice and reinforce the safety rules at all times. Role-play and rehearse "what if" scenarios.